AF484174

The Lighthouse of Prophecy

The Lighthouse of Prophecy

HENRY DERING

Copyright © 2011 International Missionary Society,

Seventh-day Adventist Church, Reform Movement,

General Conference

Copyright © 2011 IMS Publishing Association

625 West Avenue

Cedartown, GA 30125, U.S.A.

e-Mail: publishing@sda1844.org

Web site: http://www.sda1844.org

All rights reserved. No part of this book may be reproduced or transmitted in any form or by any means, electronic or mechanical, including photo-copying and storage and retrieval systems, without permission in writing of the publisher.

Photo by DesignCue on Unsplash

Printed in Georgia, U.S.A.
IMS Publishing Association
625 West Avenue
Cedartown, GA 30125,
U.S.A.

Contents

The Lighthouse of Prophecy

"We have also a more sure word of prophecy; whereunto ye do well that ye take heed, as unto a light that shineth in a dark place, until the day dawn, and the day star arise in your hearts." 2 Peter 1:19.

In the eventful and turbulent times in which we live, many thinking people are concerned about the present world condition and the secrets of the future. Those who see the world polarized between the forces of good and evil want to know what will happen next in the great battle between light and darkness. We thank God that He has not left mankind in ignorance about the course of the conflict and its outcome.

Like a great searchlight shining across the centuries, the sure word of prophecy focuses its beams upon our day. In this light we see clearly the trend of events and may understand what is coming next in the program of history fulfilling prophecy.

The Bible speaks to us of events of the past that have a lesson for the present and for the future. Prophecy is God's challenge to the infidel. One of the distinguishing characteristics of divinity is the remarkable power to foretell and record the course of history many years before the events come to pass.

In olden times, God's challenge to false religious systems was this: ". . . Declare us things for to come. Show the things that are to come hereafter, that we may know that ye are gods. . . ." Isaiah 41:22, 23. There is no god or person that can accurately reveal the future except the living God in heaven, who is able to tell the end from the beginning. "Remember the former things of old: for I am God, and there is none else; I am God, and there is none like me, declaring the end from the beginning, and from ancient times the things that are not yet done. . . ." Isaiah 46: 9, 10. By unveiling future events, the Lord has borne witness of Himself through the ages that it might be known that He rules from above all the kingdoms of men. Men thus have the opportunity to recognize His divine purpose in their lives. Besides manifesting His omnipotence in unraveling the mysteries in world affairs, God desires to shed light on His plan for man's salvation.

The fulfillment of the word of prophecy in history is a fascinating story. It is seen in matters pertaining to individuals, as well as in the affairs of cities and the great world empires. Let us examine a few examples of Bible prophecies and their unerring fulfillment.

In the dream divinely given to *Joseph,* it was revealed that his brothers would one day come as suppliants before him. His father was not pleased with the dream and said, "Shall I and thy mother and thy brethren indeed come to bow down ourselves to thee to the earth?" Genesis 37:10. Twenty years later, his brothers presented themselves before Joseph, completely unaware of his identity, and "fell before him on the ground." Genesis 44:14.

Turning our attention to *Tyre,* the greatest maritime city of antiquity, we learn that the Phoenicians traded in all the ports of the known world. All countries traded in its markets and contributed to its wealth and prosperity. Unfortunately, this majestic city was to come to a downfall. It was predicted by the prophet Ezekiel thus: "Therefore thus saith the Lord God; Behold, I am against thee, O Tyrus, and will cause many nations to come up against thee, as the sea causeth his waves to come up. And they shall destroy the walls of Tyrus, and break down her towers: I will also scrape her dust from her, and make her *like the top of a rock.* It shall be a place for the *spreading of nets* in the midst of the sea. . . ." Ezekiel 26:3-5.

This prophecy was literally fulfilled. Travelers bear witness that the site of the island city is a "rock whereon fishermen dry their nets." There is nothing to even suggest the departed glory of this once mighty metropolis.

The powerful, wealthy and apparently invincible *Babylon the Great* was doomed to be overthrown and to pass into oblivion. God foretold what nations would march against Babylon and destroy it. (Jeremiah 51:11, 28.) Fifty-seven years before Babylon fell, Jeremiah wrote two chapters of prophecy concerning its downfall. (Jeremiah 50, 51.) In the prophecy recorded in Isaiah 45:1-3, it was foretold that Cyrus would be the man who would lead the armies against Babylon. One hundred and thirteen years before he was born, the Lord called him by name!

The downfall of Babylon was accomplished by a stratagem, when it could not be done by force. It was a unique method of attack--diverting the river Euphrates which ran through the city, thus making the natural channel of the river fordable. Cyrus then was able to pass into the city without the use of battering rams or other weapons to break the mighty walls. Fifty-seven years before, God's prophet stated that this would be the method of the enemy's attack on the city. It was predicted that Cyrus would make his attack on the night of a certain Babylonian festival when the whole city would be given up to drinking and reveling. (Daniel 5.) One hundred seventy-five years before this time, Isaiah had foretold that Babylon would be given up to debauchery. (Isaiah 21:5.) Jeremiah had pointed out how the city would come to its end during the celebration. (Jeremiah 51: 39, 57.)

On the night of the feast day, Cyrus was able to go through the river gates, because the Babylonians left the lower gates open. One hundred seventy-five years before this, God had said that the gates would not be shut, and that this would contribute to success in the capture of Babylon. "Thus saith the Lord to His anointed, to Cyrus, whose right hand I have holden, to subdue nations before him; and I will loose the loins of kings, *to open before him the two-leaved gates;* and the gates shall not be shut." Isaiah 45:1. One more point of interest is the prediction that Babylon would never be rebuilt or inhabited, nor would the Arabian pitch his tent there, but the wild beasts of the desert would be there. Up to this very day, the magnificent Babylonian city remains in ruins; scarcely enough is left to mark the spot where once stood the largest, richest, and proudest city of the ancient world. Thus the history of Babylon shows us how accurately God fulfills His word. It is a positive proof of the truthfulness and reliability of the Bible.

The fulfillment of prophecy was no mere coincidence or just guesswork on the part of the writers of the Holy Word. The prophets who bore messages from God to Tyre and Babylon spoke messages also for our day. The prophetic word has much to say about events still in the future, the course of history in these last days. Rapidly the prophecies are being fulfilled, declaring the end of the world and the blessed hope of our Savior's return to earth.

Let us give heed to what that word speaks concerning our own time and thus be prepared for what is coming upon the earth.

Global Crisis Imminent

oing back in time a half dozen centuries before the birth of Christ, a proud monarch named Nebuchadnezzar ordered a gigantic golden statue to be erected on the plain of Dura in the kingdom of Babylon. It was 90 feet high and 9 feet wide! To the heathen idol worshippers this golden image was unequalled in its dazzling beauty and magnificence.

On the appointed day, a vast multitude of the most distinguished people of the empire were to assemble to worship this metallic god. At the specific command by the king, when the music band began to play, the vast assemblage of people were to fall down and thus show supreme homage to the golden god. The penalty for non-conformity was death in the fiery furnace. It was not surprising, then, that no one violated the government orders, no one, that is, except the three worthy young Hebrew men. They did not bow down for they would not transgress the commandment, "Thou shalt not make unto thee any graven image... Thou shalt not bow down thyself to them, nor serve them." Exodus 20:4, 5.

As a consequence of their unwavering faithfulness, they were cast into the furnace that had been heated seven times hotter than usual. But what happened? A miracle! The king said, "Lo, I see four men loose, walking in the midst of the fire, and they have no hurt; and the form of the fourth is like the Son of God." Daniel 3:25. What an amazing experience! God saved them from certain death. He was with them in the flames.

"Important are the lessons to be learned from the experience of the Hebrew youth on the plain of Dura. In this our day, many of God's servants, though innocent of wrongdoing, will be given over to suffer humiliation and abuse at the hands of those who, inspired by Satan, are filled with envy and religious bigotry. Especially will the wrath of man be aroused against those who hallow the Sabbath of the fourth commandment; and at last a universal decree will denounce these as deserving of death." *Prophets and Kings,* p. 512.

According to Bible prophecy, the greatest crisis in the history of this world is just before us. A decree will be passed by the governments threatening economic boycott and death to those who refuse to worship the image of the beast. The following prophetic words will soon become a reality: "And he had power to give life unto the image of the beast, that the image of the beast should both speak, and cause that as many as would not worship the image of the beast should be killed. And he causeth all, both small and great, rich and poor, free and bond, to receive a mark in their right hand, or in their foreheads: And that no man might buy or sell, save he that had the mark, or the name of the beast, or the number of his name." Revelation 13:15-17.

There is no getting around it: every person living during Earth's last hours will be faced with the decision either to obey God or to worship another power. Those who pay homage to the beast and his image will be condemned by God and receive the seven last plagues. In Revelation 14, verses 9 and 10, we read, "If any man worship the beast... and receive his mark in his forehead, or in his hand, the same shall drink of the wine of the wrath of God, which is poured out without mixture into the cup of his indignation."

This is a matter of life or death. We must know exactly what this mark is and how we can avoid it.

The mark of the beast is opposed to the seal of God. In Revelation, chapter 7, verses 2 and 3, we learn that the seal of God is placed in the forehead, just as the mark of the beast is set in the forehead. Now we ask, what is the seal? If we can define and establish this point, it will help us identify the mark.

In His Word, God tells us what His sign or seal is: "Moreover also I gave them my sabbaths, to be a sign between me and them, that they might know that I am the Lord that sanctify them." Ezekiel 20:12. Here the Sabbath is called the sign of God. Is that the same as a seal? Romans 4:11 reveals that 'seal' and 'sign' are the very same thing, being used interchangeably in the Scripture, "And he received the sign of circumcision, a seal of the righteousness of the faith which he had yet uncircumcised."

God said that the Sabbath is His sign or mark of authority. What does the beast say is the mark of its authority? Let us consider these words by C. F. Thomas, Chancellor of Cardinal Gibbons, in answer to a letter regarding the change of the Sabbath. "Of course, the Catholic church claims that the change was her act. And the act is a *mark* of her ecclesiastical power and authority in religious matters."

It is almost incredible that the majority of Christendom accepts and follows the traditions of a man-made institution.

Does anyone today have the mark of the beast? The answer is, absolutely not!

But the mark of the beast will be enforced very soon.

Therefore, in mercy, God sends out His final warning to prepare people for the coming crisis. The issue of the conflict will be whether to give God the homage or whether to obey a man-made law. In Revelation, chapter 14, verses 9 through 11, we read the most solemn warning ever given to mankind. "And the third angel followed them, saying with a loud voice, If any man worship the beast and his image, and receive his mark in his forehead, or in his hand, The same shall drink of the wine of the wrath of God, which is poured out without mixture into the cup of his indignation; and he shall be tormented with fire and brimstone in the presence of the holy angels, and in the presence of the Lamb: And the smoke of their torment ascendeth up for ever and ever: and they have no rest day nor night, who worship the beast and his image, and whosoever receiveth the mark of his name."

The counterfeit mark will not be officially received until it is enforced by the two-horned beast of Revelation 13 (America). The United States of America will become a persecuting power that will pass a national Sunday law. This act will incite other nations to follow suit. The Bible says, "...and all the world wondered after the Beast." Revelation 13:3. The whole world, except a minority of faithful souls, will observe Sunday, the child of the Papacy. Those who refuse to obey will be accused of law- breaking and of working against the state.

In order for this situation to develop, the constitution of the United States must be altered or completely abandoned. How is this possible in a land of freedom? One way is to call for a constitutional convention. It takes 34 states to request this. As of now, already 33 states are for it. Besides this movement to bring about specific changes in our fundamental laws, there are groups such as the Moral Majority Coalition, the New Liberty Federation, and the Lord's Day Alliance who have been advocating Sunday laws. The undercurrent of these voices is moving rapidly to achieve a desired goal --to get people back to going to church on Sunday.

This coercive law will seem to be the solution to the horrendous problems facing the world. "It will be declared that the nation is offending God by the violation of the Sunday-Sabbath, that this sin has brought calamities which will not cease until Sunday observance shall be strictly enforced, and that those who present the claims of the fourth commandment, thus destroying reverence for Sunday, are troublers of the nation, preventing its restoration to divine favor and temporal prosperity." *The Great Controversy*, p. 408 (1844 ed.).

According to Revelation 13:11 -16, the Protestant churches in America will be instrumental in exalting the Papal Sabbath (Sunday) and waging war against Sabbath (Saturday) keepers.

Yes, religious freedom will be taken away. Persecution will raise its ugly head again. "The Protestants of the United States will be foremost in stretching their hands across the gulf to grasp the hand of spiritualism; they will reach over the abyss to clasp hands with the Roman power; and under the influence of this threefold union, this country will follow in the steps of Rome in trampling on the rights of conscience." *The Great Controversy*, p. 588.

The ecumenical movement is taking giant steps to achieve full unity among the churches. Consider for a moment this historic event that occurred in October, 1986.

"Carrying olive branches and offering prayers, Pope John Paul II and the representatives of the world's religions, including a Crow Indian medicine man from Montana and an African animist witch doctor, pledged Monday to work for peace.

"As 60 religious leaders joined the Pope in this picturesque medieval hill town, where St. Francis preached 700 years ago, governments and rebels throughout the world put down their arms briefly in response to a papal call for a cease-fire and a day of prayer. Reflections were also offered at the retreat center by representatives of the Buddhist, Jewish, Islamic, Bahai, Sikh, Christian and native American faiths., Mormon and Quaker leaders were also involved in the day's events." *Los Angeles Times*, October 26, 1986.

Once again I quote from Revelation 13:3: "…and all the world wondered after the beast." This false unity of the churches leads to persecution, the mark of the beast, and a stupendous crisis in the world.

Another article appeared in the *New York Post* on Monday, April 14, 1986. The headline read, "N. Y. Jews, Catholics, Hail Pope's Synagogue Visit." The article said that John Cardinal O'Connor called the Pope's action "an historic move of indescribable importance."

And Pope Benedict XVI has once again reaffirmed his priority for a commitment to ecumenism which calls for "not only words but concrete gestures." In Bari, celebrating Mass to close the 24th Eucharistic Congress before 200,000 faithful, the Pope defined Sunday as a necessary instrument to leave the desert of 'frenetic consumerism, religious indifference and secularism which is closed to transcendence.' *AsiaNews.it*, May 29, 2005.

Should not these events open our eyes and alert us to what is soon coming upon the world? No matter which way you look, a great crisis is stealing upon our world. This global conflict will be like nothing man has experienced before.

According to Bible prophecy, the United States will be the primary force for enacting legislation that will cause everyone to worship the beast. Then the world will unite against those who refuse to comply with these laws.

The world is rapidly confederating under one of two masters. While ecumenism draws one block to Satan, another group is distinguished as those who "keep the commandments of God and the faith of Jesus." Revelation 14:12. With this in mind, won't we choose to obey God and keep the true Sabbath today and during the final crisis?

Signs of the End Time

These last few years the world has gone from one earth-shaking crisis to another. Many scientists warn that humanity now totters on the brink of unprecedented disaster and chaos. Day by day, the world's problems grow more desperate and insurmountable. The question which must plague every thinking person is, "What lies ahead?"

Almost two thousand years ago, looking into the future, our Lord predicted exactly what our world would be like at the end of time. What events were to happen before Jesus' return and what would be the signs of His coming and the end of the world?

INCREASED WICKEDNESS

Christ predicted that wickedness would increase prior to His return. "And because wickedness is multiplied, most men's love will grow cold." Matthew 24:12 (RSV). Jesus exemplified the pre-advent social wickedness by referring to "the days of Noah." "As it was in the days of Noah, so will it be in the days of the Son of man." Luke 17:26 (RSV).

During the days prior to the world-wide flood, mankind rejected God and tended to violence. "And God saw that the wickedness of man was great in the earth, and that every imagination of the thoughts of his heart was only evil continually. The earth also was corrupt before God, and the earth was filled with violence." Genesis 6:5, 11.

In the last days of this earth's history, there would be a repetition of the "days of Noah." Violence throughout the world would surge to unprecedented levels. We are all painfully aware of today's news full of tragic stories of senseless violence. Every day the stories get more horrible and shocking, while people are getting more desensitized to acts of unbelievable cruelty and viciousness.

- In the U.S., a teenager shoots his father because he wants to see someone bleed to death.

- In England, two ten-year-old boys kidnap and brutally murder a toddler.

- In Taiwan, four teenage boys imprison, rape and torture a fifteen-year old girl for a week and then kill her.

- In Kosovo, young and old were massacred and laid in mass graves.

- In the U.S., a six-year old boy kills another six-year old classmate with a handgun.

"This was, after all, the third multiple homicide at a Southern school in the past six months. Each successive slaughter had a progressively younger accused killer and a progressively higher body count: In Pearl, Mississippi, in October, a 16-year old shot nine students, killing two (plus his mother, with a knife); in West Paducah, Kentucky, in December, a 14-year-old killed three of his classmates and wounded five more. Last week's carnage in Jonesboro, Arkansas, may well have been the work of the youngest mass murderers in American history... When the fire alarm went off shortly after 12:30 p.m. last Tuesday, teachers and students at Westside Middle School marched dutifully outside. Four minutes and 27 bullets later, 15 bodies lay bleeding on the pavement." *U.S. News*, April 6,1998.

- On April 20, 1999, the worst high school shooting in American history happened when seniors Eric Harris and Dylan Klebold killed thirteen people, injured two dozen more and then turned their guns on themselves. www.westword.com/issues/2002-10-31

- In 2001, FBI statistics revealed that "U.S. crime rate is on the rise. The increase included a 3.1 percent rise in murders reported by police departments nationwide, along with significant jumps in the numbers of robberies, burglaries and car thefts..."

Lawlessness, violence and crime are indicators or *signs* that Jesus will be returning soon.

WARS AND RUMORS OF WARS

"And ye shall hear of wars and rumors of wars... For nation shall rise against nation, and kingdom against kingdom...." Matthew 24:6, 7.

The world has never been completely free from the scourge of war, but no period in history has witnessed the escalation of wars as has the twentieth century. The International Red Cross estimates that over 100 million people have been killed in wars since the beginning of the Twentieth Century. Just think about the most recent conflicts: the Persian Gulf War, the Somalian Conflict, the bombing of Afghanistan, and the War in Iraq. All these have been a fulfillment of the prophecy in Matthew 24:7, "Nation shall rise against nation."

Many see the prospects of another world-wide conflict. The threat of an all-out nuclear war hangs over the world. Nations such as North Korea, China, and India have weapons of mass destruction. Will the world be wiped out by a chemical, biological or nuclear war? Could this happen in our time? The Bible answer is, "Absolutely NOT!" It will be Jesus who will destroy the wicked and then set up His kingdom on the New Earth.

PREACHING THE GOSPEL

"And this gospel of the kingdom shall be preached in all the world for a witness unto all nations; and then shall the end come."

Never has the gospel been preached in *all* the world to *all* nations as it is now. If not directly by missionaries, it is certainly being preached through the modern media--radio, television, and the world wide web.

The gospel has been preached to over four billion people. Statistics on the translation and distribution of the Bible reveal the growth of the gospel witness. Over 50 million Bibles, as well as nearly 80 milllion New Testaments, are distributed every year. The entire Bible or parts thereof, having been translated partially or entirely into some 2,092 different languages and dialects, are now available to about 98 percent of the world's population.

The world will end when every living person has heard the good news--the gospel of Jesus Christ. It won't be much longer before 100 percent of the world will have heard the message of salvation.

NATURAL DISASTERS

"And there shall be signs in the sun, and in the moon, and in the stars; and upon the earth distress of nations, with perplexity; the sea and the waves roaring." Luke 21:25.

"In the United States, over 200 tornadoes were observed in January, nearly 14 times the average number... Through November, the U.S. experienced the second greatest number of tornadoes on record, following 1998's recent year." *National Oceanic and Atmospheric Administration and National Climatic Data Center.*

"After a string of tornadoes killed dozens and turned life upside down for tens of thousands of people in their path, residents of Kansas, Missouri and Tennessee try to clean up while bracing for the possibility of more twisters." *MSNBC News* May 6, 2003.

"Large scale natural disasters are three times as common as they were in the 1960s experts said yesterday as they declared 1998 the most calamitous on record. Comparing the figures for the 1960s and the past ten years, we have established that the number of great natural catastrophes was three times larger." *The Times*: World News, December 30, 1998.

Disasters appear to have increased significantly in recent years. Nature has gone berserk This clearly indicates that Jesus is coming again soon!

FAMINES AND PESTILENCES

"And there shall be famines and pestilences." Matthew 24:7. Famines have occurred many times in the history of this world, but they have not occurred on the scale with which they have in the Twentieth Century. Never before has the world had millions of people suffering from starvation or malnutrition. Jesus predicted that there would be an abundance of plagues and diseases marking the time of His return.

The medical community is now warning that not only are bacterial plagues on the rise, but viral killers like HIV and Ebola are occurring more frequently than ever. The World Health Organization states, ""Around the world, more than 6,000 people every day are infected with the HIV and the epidemic is getting worse." Researchers have not found a cure for HIV. Malawi, like many African countries, is on the cusp of famine and every day new graves are being dug for those who have died of hunger. The combination of severe food shortages and the killer HIV is set to destroy many communities across southern Africa unless help arrives soon. Nearly 13 million people in six southern African countries are at risk of starvation." *"Crisis Looms in Africa"* http://edition.cnn.com/2002/WORLD/africa/06/11/famine.charity/ June 11, 2002.

Mention must also be made of the deadly SARS (Severe Acute Respiratory Syndrome). This epidemic has caused panic, misery and death in various parts of the world, and it is still not contained.

Are not the frequent famines and the incurable diseases indicators that this generation is living in the end times?

RELIGIOUS DECLINE

The widespread proclamation of the gospel does not necessarily mean a massive growth in genuine Christianity. Instead, the Bible predicts a decline of true spirituality toward the end of time. Apostle Paul wrote that "in the last days perilous times shall come. For men shall be lovers of their own selves, covetous, boasters, proud, blasphemers, disobedient to parents, unthankful, unholy, without natural affection, truce breakers, false accusers, incontinent, fierce, despisers of those that are good, traitors, heady, highminded, lovers of pleasures more than lovers of God; having a form of godliness, but denying the power thereof: from such turn away." 2 Timothy, 3:1-5.

So today, love of self, material things and the world has supplanted the Spirit of Christ in many hearts.

According to Bible prophecy, the signs of the times clearly and boldly declare the greatest event in history— the second coming of Jesus--to be imminent. Are we preparing ourselves for this momentous event?

"Watch therefore: for ye know not what hour your Lord doth come. Therefore be ye also ready: for in such an hour as ye think not, the Son of man cometh." Matthew 24:42, 44.

Now is the time for us to go to Jesus and let Him purify our sinful hearts. "All that the Father giveth me shall come to me; and him that cometh to me I will in no wise cast out." John 6:37.

Doomsday

Is the world headed for total destruction? Will it come to a sudden end in our time? I think you will agree that these are serious, thought-provoking questions.

For many the future looks dark and without hope. Military leaders often see blackness sweeping across the western sky. Their prediction is the final battle of *Armageddon* and the annihilation of the human race. Environmentalists are forecasting the strangulation of our sick and fragile planet. Little hope is offered to cure the cancer that has seeped into our air, water and land masses. There appear to be no solutions for the earth's troubles.

The gigantic and unsolvable problems of Mother Nature are running wild, and no one seems to be able to control the natural disasters. Every year thousands of people lose their lives in earthquakes, tornadoes, floods and hurricanes. Then there are the toxic waste problems, acid rain, the greenhouse effect (the rise in temperature that the Earth experiences because certain gases in the atmosphere trap energy from the sun) weakening the ozone layer, the pollution of our oceans, lakes and rivers. Furthermore, there are problems and hot spots that plague the world. Africa explodes with AIDS and famines; Asia burns with overpopulation and a low standard of living. The Middle East boils with constant eruptions of strife and bloodshed. North America battles a steady, rising tide of lawlessness and immorality.

What a dreadful world--out of control and ready to split at the seams! World conditions have never been grimmer. The storm clouds are here to stay. They shower their lethal dosage of pain, sorrow and death. Things are bad. In fact, it will get worse before it gets better. Yes, it will get better! There is a definite promise of better things to come. There is hope for you and me.

The answer and solution to all the world's multitude of problems is Jesus-Christ!

Jesus said that this sin-filled world must run its course at full-throttle and then He will come again to clean up the man-made mess. The Bible gives us the comforting assurance of a complete restoration--everything will become brand new. But you ask, when? Read carefully the following, "And there shall be signs in the sun, and in the moon and in the stars; and upon the earth distress of nations, with perplexity; the sea and the waves roaring; men's hearts failing them for fear, and for looking after those things which are coming on the earth: for the powers of heaven shall be shaken. And then shall they see the Son of man coming in a cloud with power and great glory. And when these things begin to come to pass, then look up, and lift up your heads, for your redemption draweth nigh." Luke 21:25-28.

The second coming of Jesus is a definite promise that Christians can rest upon. Some predict that the world will come to an end in the year 2011 A.D. But does anyone really know the *exact* time?

Jesus speaks to us today in Matthew 24:36, 42: "But of that day and hour knoweth no man, no, not the angels of heaven, but my Father only. Watch therefore: for ye know not what hour your Lord doth come."

In the same chapter Jesus tells us some intriguing facts about His second coming and the end of civilization. Now let's continue to search the sacred pages of the Word of God to find out more about this prophecy. Let us personally examine particular areas that clearly indicate the time inwhich we are living.

Signs of the Times

Jesus said emphatically that one outstanding sign of the times would be

WARS

We read the following in Matthew, chapter 24, verses 6 and 7: "And ye shall hear of wars and rumours of wars: see that ye be not troubled: for all these things must come to pass, but the end is not yet. For nation shall rise against nation, and kingdom against kingdom."

The prophet Joel writes about the preparations for last day conflicts. Here are his words: "...Prepare war, wake up the mighty men, let all the men of war draw near; let them come up: Beat your plowshares into swords.... let the weak say I am strong." Joel 3, 9, 10.

The super powers, wealthy nations, and even some of the third world countries are arming themselves for an all-out conflict. Weaker nations have developed nuclear weapons and are now saying, "I am strong."

The prospect of a nuclear holocaust seems to be balancing on a tightrope. Most statesmen, military leaders, historians and scientists think that we are inches away from an all-out catastrophe. In recent times there have been international border violations, planes shot down, ships fired on, diplomatic ultimatums, and undeclared or limited wars fought.

WHAT IS IT ALL LEADING UP TO?

Does the possibility exist for terrorists to obtain and use nuclear weapons? Of course, no one can with certainty rule this out. A mad terrorist could accidentally or willfully push the button, turn the key, and launch a missile with a nuclear warhead. Does this sound frightening to you? Could such an insane act trigger World War III? And what would be our chances of surviving?

And consider for a moment all the sophisticated weaponry that America has and its potential to kill!

Besides these terrifying conventional means of destroying life, there "are even uglier ways to kill--chemical and biological warfare. Here is a description of the various methods and horrors of these weapons: "The next generation of terror weapons could come from the laboratories of biologists. Souped up by genetic engineering, bacteria, viruses and toxins could be used to spread cure-resistant forms of such diseases as anthrax or cholera, or to mass-produce the killing effects of botulism or the bite of a rattlesnake." *Newsweek*, January 16, 1989.

In addition to biological weapons, there is the threat of poison gases (chemical warfare): tear gas, vomit gas, mustard gas, blood gas, and nerve gas.

The potential effects of these ugly weapons are just too terrible to contemplate. Man's inhumanity to man is almost incomprehensible.

History is again repeating itself, especially the days of Noah. Genesis 6:5 and 11 describes the conditions of the earth just before the world-wide flood. "And God saw that the wickedness of man was great in the earth, and that every imagination of the thoughts of his heart was only evil continually. The earth also was corrupt before God, and the earth was filled with violence."

Are we not repeating the sins of Noah's time? What does all this mean to you, dear reader? To me, it means that Jesus Christ will soon be coming back to this earth. But before this great event takes place, our loving God will warn this world to repent and turn to Him.

God's Word says that there is not much time left for the inhabitants of the world to return to Him. The Doomsday Clock, symbolizing the threat of nuclear doom, is quickly approaching midnight.

Are you fearful of a nuclear holocaust that will annihilate every man, woman and child? Don't be afraid, dear friend. This will never happen. According to the

Bible it will be Jesus Christ who will destroy this world, and not man. This takes place when He comes back to this earth. Consider these words found in 2 Thess. 1:7-9. "And to you who are troubled rest with us, when the Lord Jesus shall be revealed from heaven with his mighty angels, in flaming fire taking vengeance on them that know not God, and that obey not the gospel of our Lord Jesus Christ: Who shall be punished with everlasting destruction from the presence of the Lord, and from the glory of his power." What a blessed hope for the Christian and what a fearful end for the unbeliever!

EARTHQUAKES

"...And there shall be earthquakes, in divers places." Matt. 24:7.

Earthquakes are a direct fulfillment of our Savior's prophecy. We may expect that they will become more frequent and more destructive as we near the end. History tells us that such has been the case as shown by the following statements of facts.

In the Sixteenth Century, there were 253 earthquakes; in the Eighteenth Century--640 earthquakes, and in the Nineteenth Century--2119 earthquakes. In our century we constantly hear of the destructive nature of earthquakes. They have become so severe and so frequent that they have killed more than a million people since World War II alone.

"In the last 15 years, nearly 500,000 people have died in earthquakes--more than in any other type of natural disaster." *Life* magazine, February 1989, p. 40.

In 1985 more than 10,000 people died in the Mexican devastation. Then in December 1988 in Armenia, "As many as 100,000 of Leninakan's 290,000 residents were dead, by unofficial estimates. At least 20,000 more died in Spitak and other Armenian towns." *Newsweek,* December 26, 1988, p. 32. "At least 500,000 people were said to be homeless...." *Newsweek,* December 19, 1988, p. 19. A 7.9-magnitude earthquake devastated central China, with the death toll exceeding 65,000 and 5 million left homeless, as of May 26, 2008. This was the country's worst earthquake in three decades.

The Hour of Judgment is Come

Charles G. Finney, a young lawyer, sat in a village law office in New York one morning. All alone, he seemed to hear a voice:

"Finney, what are you going to do when you finish your schooling?"

"Why, put out my shingle and practice law, I imagine."

"Then what?"

"Build a big, beautiful house and have a family—after I develop my law firm, of course."

"What next?"

"Well, I'll grow old and retire."

"Then what?"

"I'll die."

"And then?"

"The judgment."

Finney recalled a text from childhood: "It is appointed unto men once to die, but after this the judgment."[1] As he contemplated the solemn thought of a judgment to come, he surrendered his heart to God—and a profound change took place in Finney's life.

Do you realize that you, too, must face the judgment? "For we must all appear before the judgment seat of Christ; that every one may receive the things done in his body, according to that he hath done, whether it be good or bad."[2] No one will be overlooked, and no one is exempt from this judgment. God will judge man, not men their fellow men. Think for a moment. Someday your whole life will be reviewed before the entire universe. Everyone will know what you really are. Does that make you feel uncomfortable, perhaps afraid? If so, do something before it is too late. Prepare now to be pronounced "not guilty."

When does the judgment take place? Well, one judgment precedes the second coming of Christ. It determines whether you will be saved or lost. "Wait a minute," you may say. "I thought the judgment takes place *after* Christ's coming." Let me explain. The judgment has three phases. The first phase, the investigative judgment, pertains to all who have ever professed to be followers of Christ and determines whether or not their names will be retained in the book of life.

The second phase takes place during the millennium, the 1,000-year period after Christ has taken the righteous to heaven. During that time, the righteous will investigate the records of the unrighteous and pronounce sentence on them.

The execution of those sentences takes place during phase three of the judgment. "And fire came down from God out of heaven, and devoured them. ... And death and hell were cast into the lake of fire. This is the second death."[3] In this article I will focus on the judgment that precedes the second coming of Christ, the deliberations that began in 1844 (as pinpointed in Daniel 8).

At this moment, then, the investigative judgment is taking place. Writing about our generation, John the Revelator urged us to "Fear God, and give glory to him; for the hour of his judgment is come."[4] Not "may come" or "will come" but "is come." What does this mean? It means that the investigative judgment is *now* in session in heaven. For 164 years, the judge, jury, witnesses, and defense attorney have been at work.

Come with me. Let's review this heavenly court scene. "I beheld till the thrones were cast down, and the Ancient of days did sit, whose garment was white as snow, and the hair of his head like the pure wool: his throne was like the fiery flame, and his wheels as burning fire. A fiery stream issued and came forth from before him: thousand thousands ministered unto him, and ten thousand times ten thousand stood before him: the judgment was set, and the *books were opened.*"[5] (Emphasis supplied.)

Here we see God, the Judge, sitting upon His throne. Before Him are thousands and thousands of angels who serve as faithful witnesses. In today's earthly courts of justice, mistakes are made. A fact may be omitted or distorted, a jury biased. What would result? An unfair trial, in which an innocent man is convicted of a crime he did not commit, or a guilty woman is set free. This will not happen when God does the final judging. His ways are righteous and perfect.

The Bible describes the records used in the judgment. "The books were opened: and another book was opened, which is the *book of life*: and the dead were judged out of those things which were written in the books, according to their works."[6] (Emphasis supplied.)

The book of life, then, is one of the opened books. It is absolutely essential for a person's name to appear in this book in order to be saved. Any time anyone accepts Jesus as Savior, that person's name is recorded in the book of life.

There is, however, very definitely a possibility of one's name being blotted out of the book of life. The Bible does not teach "once saved, always saved." Yes, you *can* fall away from grace if you are not faithful till the end of your life. "He that overcometh," wrote John, "the same shall be clothed in white raiment; and I will not blot out his name out of the book of life."[7]

The investigative judgment began with the first name in the book of life—Adam. Next to his name is written "pardon." Although Adam sinned, he truly repented and accepted the precious blood of Christ in his behalf. Adam's name remained in the heavenly record book. Abel's name was also called in the investigative judgment. Because he, too, trusted in God, Abel's name is still in the Lamb's book of life. Many centuries later, Judas became a follower of Jesus. Judas, however, lost his place in the book of life because he sold his Master for 30 pieces of silver.

How sad, how terrible to have your name removed from such an important record! No longer eligible for eternal life, you are now doomed to eternal death. One of these days, very soon, my name will be called in the heavenly tribunal. If you believe in Christ, your case, too, will be considered. Have you repented of every sin and asked Jesus to forgive you?

Malachi speaks of another heavenly volume, the book of remembrance.[8] This contains all the good deeds performed by the righteous. "There every temptation resisted, every evil overcome, every word of tender pity expressed, is faithfully chronicled."[9]

Every time we yield to temptation, however, our sin is accurately recorded in another place, the book of sin.[10] The holy angels sadly witness every wayward act. Not only do they record our visible actions, but our deepest thoughts are registered as well. God looks directly into our hearts. He sees our envy, our lust, even when no one else guesses that such feelings exist—or realizes to what they may lead. "Whosoever looketh on a woman to lust after her," Jesus clearly stated, "hath committed adultery with her already in his heart."[11]

We cannot fool or deceive God. Not ever. "Sin may be concealed," wrote an inspired author. It may be "denied, covered up from father, mother, wife, children, and associates; no one but the guilty actors may cherish the least suspicion of the wrong; but it is laid bare before the intelligences of heaven. The darkness of the darkest night, the secrecy of all deceptive acts, is not sufficient to veil one thought from the knowledge of the Eternal."[12] Long before, wise Solomon had written that "God shall bring every work into judgment, with every secret thing, whether it be good or whether it be evil."[13]

By what standard will each of us be judged? Our deeds will be measured by conformance to God's holy and perfect law, the Ten Commandments. As the apostle James warns, "So speak ye, and so do, as they that shall be judged by the *law of liberty.*"[14] (Emphasis supplied.) Imagine! God's law is described as the "law of liberty." Although the Ten Commandments reveal our sins and condemn us to death, they also make us realize our need for a Savior. Jesus came to this earth for only one reason: to save us from eternal death. "If we confess our sins, he is faithful and just to forgive us our sins, and to cleanse us from all unrighteousness."[15] What a marvelous promise!

In your heavenly day in court, who will represent you? Who is your defense attorney, your personal lawyer, your advocate? "My little children," wrote John in yet another message of entreaty, "these things write I unto you, that ye sin not. And if any man sin, we have an advocate with the Father, Jesus Christ the righteous."[16]

This very day, Jesus pleads His merits on behalf of His faithful children. Standing before the Father, Christ confidently says, "My blood, Father; My blood is sufficient for them." What a wonderful defense attorney we have!

Very soon, however, Jesus will end His work as our Advocate. The last name called, the books will be shut, the court will close forever. "He that is unjust, let him be unjust still: and he which is filthy, let him be filthy still: and he that is righteous, let him be righteous still: and he that is holy, let him be holy still."[17] At this pronouncement, the verdict of the trial for every human being that has ever lived will have been decided innocent—or guilty.

"The hour of His judgment," I repeat, "is come."[4]

Court is in session. Some names are being cleared; others, condemned. Today, accept Jesus as your Savior, your Advocate. He loves you; He died to save you. Now this moment, confess your sins to Him like Charles Finney did. Jesus will forgive and defend you. He *will* win your case.

ENDNOTES

1. Hebrews 9:27
2. 2 Corinthians 5:10
3. Revelation 20:9, 14
4. Revelation 14:7
5. Daniel 7:9-10
6. Revelation 20:12
7. Revelation 3:5
8. Malachi 3:16
9. *The Great Controversy,* p. 481
10. Psalm 51:1, 9; Isaiah 43:25
11. Matthew 5:28
12. *The Great Controversy,* p. 486
13. Ecclesiastes 12:14
14. James 2:12
15. 1 John 1:9
16. 1 John 2:1
17. Revelation 22:11

The Seven Trumpets

In chapters 8 and 9 of the book of Revelation, the Lord portrays another most interesting viewpoint of His plan in history. These trumpets retrace to a great extent the period already covered by the seven churches and the seven seals. They show that God's messages to His people throughout time were combined with justice and mercy in punishing evil. It is God who sends seven judgments upon apostate Christians—those who were the persecutors of God's true people. The trumpets describe the principal political and military events during the Christian era directed against the western and eastern Roman Empire. Though they are in the past, still they hold great significance, as they clearly show how God is in control of all the events of this world. Let us see how these prophesied events, which are described to us in strange-sounding symbolic language, were fulfilled. To understand how these events took place, we must look at history.

"The first angel sounded, and there followed hail and fire mingled with blood, and they were cast upon the earth: and the third part of trees was burnt up, and all green grass was burnt up." Revelation 8:7. Thus is symbolized the first trumpet or judgment which fell upon the western part of the Roman Empire, the portion that rejected God and His love. It was an invasion by the Goths, a barbarian tribe from the frozen regions of the North, under the leadership of Alaric. This is the reason the symbol of hail was used in the prophecy. This barbaric incursion occurred about the close of the fourth century and onward. The invaders overran Macedonia, Thrace, Greece, and then crossed the Alps and pillaged and set fire to the city of Rome in A.D. 410.

"Many cities were cruelly oppressed, or destroyed. Many thousands were inhumanly massacred. The consuming flames of war spread over the greatest part of the seventeen provinces of Gaul.

"Alaric again stretched his ravages over Italy. During four years the Goths ravaged and reigned over it without control. And in the pillage and fire of Rome, the streets of the city were filled with dead bodies. . . ." Uriah Smith, *Daniel and the Revelation,* pp. 477, 478.

How terrible was the retribution of God upon sinners who had rejected His love! It seemed as if almost every living thing was to be destroyed. "And the second angel sounded, and as it were a great mountain burning with fire was cast into the sea: and the third part of the sea became blood; And the third part of the creatures which were in the sea, and had life, died; and the third part of the ships were destroyed." Revelation 8:8, 9.

The next act of invasion which broke up the Roman Empire was by Genseric and his Vandals. This symbolism reveals a warfare at sea rather than upon land. By establishing his headquarters on the north African coast around Carthage, he was able to dominate the Mediterranean with a navy of pirates, pillaging the coasts of Spain, Italy and Greece and preying upon Roman commerce. Our word "vandalism" gives us an idea of what his actions were like. The "third part" mentioned in the verses above refers to the division of the Roman Empire after Constantine's death among his three sons. In our prophecy we deal with the third of the Roman Empire given to Constans, mainly Africa and Italy. A desperate attempt by the Romans to wipe out the Vandals only saw Genseric reestablish himself as the sovereign of the seas. His ships of war and barges filled with combustible material set on fire and destroyed the Roman fleet of 1,113 ships and over 100,000 men. It was a literal fulfillment of the burning mountain being cast into the sea as the Roman fleet went up in flames.

The judgments of God were not finished yet. "And the third angel sounded, and there fell a great star from heaven, burning as it were a lamp, and it fell upon the third part of the rivers, and upon the fountains of waters; And the name of the star is called Wormwood: and the third part of the waters became wormwood; and many men died of the waters, because they were made bitter." Revelation 8:10, 11.

In the interpretation of these scripture verses, the star called Wormwood is a symbol of Attila and his Huns who invaded the Roman Empire. He appeared suddenly like a blazing star and then vanished like a star whose light was quenched in the waters. The areas that he made "bitter" or devastated were the regions of the Alps and those portions of the empire whence the rivers flow down into Italy. "It was the boast of Attila that the grass never grew on the spot which his horse had trod. 'The scourge of God' was a name that he appropriated to himself, and inserted among his royal titles. He was 'the scourge of his enemies, and the terror of the world.'"—*Daniel and the Revelation*, p. 485.

Even this great devastation did not bring the people to repentance toward God. Therefore, He permitted an additional calamity to befall them. "And the fourth angel sounded, and the third part of the sun was smitten, and the third part of the moon, and the third part of the stars; so as the third part of them was darkened, and the day shone not for a third part of it, and the night likewise." Revelation 8:12.

In the sixth century the Heruli, another barbarian tribe under Odoacer, dethroned the last emperor and extinguished the imperial glory of the Western Empire. The symbols "sun, moon and stars" denote the great luminaries of the Roman government—its emperors, senators and consuls that were brought to extinction. Fearful were the calamities brought about by the barbaric invasions, but they were light as compared with what was to follow.

The next three trumpets are called woes because of the more terrible events to take place under their sounding. The Moslem world—the Saracens and the Turks—became a scourge of the apostate Roman Catholic Church which had usurped the remains of the Roman Empire. The fifth angel sounded and out of the wilderness of Arabia the followers of Mohammed arose like smoke out of a pit to torment the Eastern Empire especially. Revelation 9:1, 2.

They were commanded to torment those who did not have the seal of God in their foreheads. In other words, their attacks were to be directed only against unrighteous men. They hurt the apostate Catholic Church which was destroying the people of God. Abu-Bakr, Mohammed's successor, said to his soldiers: "You will find another sort of people that belong to the synagogue of Satan, who have shaven crowns; be sure you cleave their skulls, and give them no quarter, till they either turn Mahometans or pay 'tribute.'" — *Daniel and the Revelation,* p. 498.

On July 27, 1299, Othman I, the traditional founder of the Ottoman Empire, made his first assault on the Greek division of the Eastern Roman Empire. 150 years later the Greek empire was still independent and was not conquered, in fulfillment of the prophecy of Revelation 9:5, that they should be tormented for five months. This time period was fulfilled exactly. Five months at 30 days each = 150 days. Because in Bible prophecy one day = one year (see Numbers 14:34; Ezekiel 4:6), this torment was to last 150 years. This woe depicted trouble but not total destruction.

Much could be said regarding the literal fulfillment of the other aspects of this prophecy, but space does not allow. Since, however, even these great and terrible happenings were not heeded by the people, additional troubles had to come to bring the prophecies to a complete fulfillment. The prophecies of God's Word will always be completed. Note the words of God, "And the sixth angel sounded, and I heard a voice from the four horns of the golden altar which is before God. Saying to the sixth angel which had the trumpet, Loose the four angels which are bound in the great river Euphrates. And the four angels were loosed, which were prepared for an hour, and a day, and a month, and a year, for to slay the third part of men." Revelation 9:13-15. Here is another specific time prophecy—1 hour, 1 day, 1 month, 1 year. Under the second woe (the sixth trumpet), the Lord used the Turks to punish the apostate Christian world. A new mode of warfare was introduced—gunpowder, firearms and cannon—that was used by the Turks in their warfare against the Eastern Empire.

"It was to 'the fire and the smoke and the sulphur,' to the artillery and firearms of Mahomet, that the killing of the third part of men, i.e., the capture of Constantinople, and by consequence the destruction of the Greek Empire, was owing." — *Daniel and the Revelation,* p. 510.

The time period of this prophecy was not understood until the year 1838, when Josiah Litch published a complete explanation of Revelation 9. From his calculations of the Biblical prophecy, he predicted that the Ottoman Empire would lose its independence "in A.D. 1840, sometime in the month of August." —Ellen G. White, *The Great Controversy,* p. 334. Just a few days before the event, he even predicted the exact day on which this would take place.

His calculations were based on the following figures: The 150 years of the previous woe began on July 27, 1299, and extended to July 27, 1449. At this time the prophetic period of "an hour, and a day, and a month, and a year" began. When we apply again the prophetic yardstick of one day = one year, we come to the following conclusions:

1 hour =15 days
1 day = 1 year
1 month of 30 days = 30 years
1 year of 360 days = 360 years

Total =391 years and 15 days

With the starting point of July 27, 1449, this time period would extend to August 11, 1840. On that very day the Turkish Sultan put his affairs into the hands of the great powers—England, Russia, Austria and Prussia; and thus Ottoman independence was gone. The time set for the fulfillment of this prophecy by Josiah Litch was watched with great interest by thousands. When it was fulfilled, much strength was given to the Advent Message which Josiah Litch helped to preach.

The line of trumpets seems to be interrupted by another event—a great proclamation of God described as an angel coming down from heaven to earth. His message is proclaimed to all parts of the earth; "and he set his right foot upon the sea and his left foot on the earth." This message is to go even to the furthest island of the sea. In this way every person on earth will be left without excuse.

No more prophetic time is to be given. "There should be time no longer." We are living on borrowed time. Very soon the mystery of God will be finished, the seven last plagues will fall, and Jesus will come. Probationary time for each person on earth will be over. Are you ready for the final judgment?

The Third Angel's Message

The most fearful threatening ever addressed to mortals is contained in the third angel's message found in Revelation 14:9-11: "And the third angel followed them, saying with a loud voice, If any man worship the beast and his image, and receive his mark in his forehead, or in his hand, the same shall drink of the wine of the wrath of God, which is poured out without mixture into the cup of his indignation..."

It is a solemn warning to you and me, dear friend. It is a warning to everyone on this earth. To worship the beast, the image, and to receive the mark of the beast means to receive the wrath of God. The wrath of God is contained in the seven last plagues, which are reserved for the ungodly, and not for the obedient righteous. God protects His people during the outpouring of His wrath.

Who is this beast mentioned in Revelation 14?

Is it some charismatic person who has the power to perform wonders and miracles?

Is it a sophisticated computer in Switzerland that issues cards bearing the number 666?

Is it Communist China?

Who is the Beast??

I believe we need to know for sure. Wouldn't you agree? We cannot just speculate, since it is a life-and-death matter.

God describes the beast in chapter 13 of the book of Revelation, and gives us some characteristics by which to identify the beast.

Let us prayerfully study our Bibles so that we can determine who this beast is. God wants us to be informed and to know. He doesn't want us to perish.

In Revelation 13:1, John describes a beast coming up out o the sea having 7 heads with names of blasphemy written on them. It also has 10 horns with crowns upon them. That sure is a strange kind of beast. What does it all mean to you, dear friend?

A beast in Bible prophecy represents a power or kingdom. (Daniel 7:23.)

Verse 2 of Revelation, chapter 13 further describes this beast. "And the beast which I saw was like unto a leopard, and his feet were as the feet of a bear, his mouth as the mouth of a lion."

Who is this beast?

From all the information that is given to us in this chapter and other facts found in the book of Daniel, we come to the conclusion that this beast is none other than the papal system. Prophecy speaks about the system, not the individual believers of the organization.

What characteristics does the Bible cite that lead us to conclude that the beast is the papal system? Let's examine some of these identifying specifications.

In Revelation 13:5 we read that the beast was to blaspheme against God. What is the meaning of blasphemy? In John 10:33 Jesus was accused of blasphemy by the Pharisees, because He claimed to be God. And in Matthew 9:13, He was accused because He claimed to have the power to forgive sins. Jesus could not have committed the sin of blasphemy since He is God and can forgive.

Now then, is there anyone in the religious world who is guilty of blasphemy? Do we find anyone claiming to be God? Consider, please, these statements from Catholic sources which reveal the attitude of the church on this subject.

"In 1335 Bishop Alvarez Pelayo lays down the doctrine that as Christ partook of the nature of God and man, so the Pope... is not simply a man, but rather a God on Earth." Henry C. Lea, *Studies in Church History*, p. 389.

Here is another statement:

"The Pope is not only the representative of Jesus Christ, but He is Jesus Christ Himself, hidden under the veil of flesh." *The Catholic National,* July 1895.

I'd like to present another statement found in *The Convert's Catechism of Catholic Doctrine,* page 27: We read:

"Question: Who is the Holy Father or Pope?

Answer: The Holy Father or Pope is the Visible Head of the Church, the Successor of St. Peter and the Vicar of Christ on earth." Vicar means "a substitute or the one in the place of."

Besides these claims, the papacy also claims to have power to forgive sinners. Is this a fact or just hearsay? Let's see. Turning to Geiermann's *Catechism,* p. 81, we read.

"Question: What is confession?

Answer: Confession is the telling of our sins to the priest of God to obtain forgiveness."

The Pope is the vicar of Christ...The claims of the Pope are the same as the claims of Christ... Christ can forgive all sin. So can the Pope." *Syracuse Post-Standard,* March 14, 1912.

Yet another statement: "The priest not only declares that the sinner is forgiven, but He really forgives Him... So great is the power of the priest that the judgments of Heaven itself are subject to his decision." Rev. Michael Mueller in *'The Catholic Priest.'*

Another identifying characteristic is found in Revelation 13:18. This verse deals with the number 666. It is interesting and significant to note that one of the titles of the Pope of Rome is Vicarius Filii Dei. It is a Latin title and means Vicar of the Son of God. The numerical value of the letters comprising the words Vicarius Filii Dei add up to 666, just as the Bible indicated. (V is Roman numeral 5; I is 1; C is one hundred, etc.)

Still another identifying characteristic of this beast is found in Daniel 7:25. "And he shall speak great words against the most High, and shall wear out the saints of the most High, and think to change times and laws." Do we know of any person or organization that has admitted to having changed the law of God? Remember, dear reader, God's moral law as shown in the 10 commandments can never be changed, but someone can *think* to change them. Papal Rome admits that it has changed God's rest day, the 7th day Sabbath, to Sunday, a man-made institution.

Can I prove this fact from a Catholic publication? *The Convert's Catechism of Catholic Doctrine,* by Peter Geierman, p. 50:

"Question: Which is the Sabbath day?

Answer: Saturday is the Sabbath day.

Question: Why do we observe Sunday instead of Saturday?

Answer: We observe Sunday instead of Saturday because the Catholic Church, in the Council of Laodicea (A.D. 336) transferred the Solemnity from Saturday to Sunday." These words are clear and they leave no doubt or question in our minds.

Now you may be wondering what the Protestant churches have to say about the Sabbath day. This is what the Congregationalists say: "It is quite clear that however rigidly or devotedly we may spend Sunday, we are not keeping the Sabbath...The Sabbath was founded on a specific, divine command. We can plead no such command for the observance of Sunday. There is not a single line in the New Testament to suggest that we incur any penalty by violating the supposed sanctity of Sunday." Dr. R. W. Dale, *The Ten Commandments*, pp.106-107.

What do the Presbyterians say? "There is no word, no hint in the New Testament about abstaining from work on Sunday. The observance of Ash Wednesday, or Lent, stands exactly on the same footing as the observance of Sunday. Into the rest of Sunday no Divine Law enters." Canon Eyton, in *The Ten Commandments*.

What do the Anglicans say? "And where are we told to keep the first day at all? We are commanded to keep the seventh; but we are nowhere commanded to keep the first day." Isaac Williams, *Plain Sermons on the Catechism*, pp. 334-336.

I will not quote what the Baptists, the Lutherans, Free Church, Episcopalians, Methodists, Disciples of Christ, and the Southern Baptists say. They all write in their books that the change from Saturday to Sunday is not warranted by the Bible.

Friends, look into the subject more thoroughly. Read your Bible to see whether God has authorized a change of the Sabbath. You will not find it.

At this time you may be wondering about the Mark of the Beast. What does it mean?

Turning to Revelation 13 we learn that Persecution will raise its ugly head in the United States. Those who are faithful will not be able to buy or sell. This means that they will not be permitted to purchase the basic necessities to sustain life. Your local supermarket will deny you food, unless you are a worshipper of the beast. You will not be able to buy gas for your car, clothing, furniture or anything else, unless you are a worshipper of the beast. Sounds preposterous? Not at all!

Our freedoms will disappear, especially the freedom to worship according to the dictates of our conscience.

There will be terrible times in the United States. The national government will unite with the churches to enforce a strict Sunday law. It will demand that we worship on Sunday. "Those who honor the Bible Sabbath will be denounced as enemies of law and order, as breaking down the moral restraints of society, causing anarchy and corruption, and calling down the judgments of God upon the earth. The conscientious scruples will be pronounced obstinacy, stubbornness and contempt of authority. They will be accused of disaffection toward the government. Ministers who deny the obligation of the divine law will present from the pulpit the duty of yielding obedience to the civil authorities as ordained of God. In legislative halls and courts of justice, commandment-keepers will be misrepresented and condemned. A false coloring will be given to their words; the worst construction will be put upon their motives." *The Great Controversy*, p. 592.

Friends, we are headed toward a crisis. The man-made institution of Sunday will be exalted and people will be expected to give reverence to this day. However, there will be a minority who will be faithful to God and who will keep the true Sabbath-day--Saturday.

You may have to stand seemingly all alone in this soon-to-come battle, but your fidelity will be richly rewarded.

Now is the time to prepare for the final test. Now is the time to awake. Now is the time to keep all the Ten Commandments. John the Revelator says: 'Blessed are they that do his commandments, that they may have right to the tree of life, and may enter in through the gates into the city." Revelation 22:14.

The Beast, His Image, and His Mark

"The third angel followed them, saying with a loud voice, If any man worship the beast and his image, and receive his mark in his forehead, or in his hand, The same shall drink of the wine of the wrath of God, which is poured out without mixture into the cup of his indignation; and he shall be tormented with fire and brimstone in the presence of the holy angels, and in the presence of the Lamb: And the smoke of their torment ascendeth up for ever and ever: and they have no rest day nor night, who worship the beast and his image, and whosoever receiveth the mark of his name." Revelation 14: 9–11.

Let us imagine someone walking into a grocery store to buy some food. The owner of the store has replaced the product-scanning machine with a body scanner. The scanner picks up the information stored in the microchip that was recently implanted in the customer's right hand, following the passing of a new national law. The chip signals whether the customer will be allowed to purchase anything. Like the photograph on a driver's license, the data on the chip provide information vital to national security: a person's name, address, date of birth, medical history, church affiliation and, last, whether he/she supports the new world order.

Others speculate that the antichrist will engrave visible marks or tattoos in the foreheads or right hands to identify his subjects. Will social security numbers be used to track down supposed enemies and subject them to imprisonment or death? Could these things actually happen in the future? Is this really what the Bible says about the mark of the beast?

There is so much speculation about the beast, his image, and his mark. What is the truth about this subject? Let us try to unravel some things that appear to be mysteries in the book of Revelation.

IDENTIFYING THE BEAST

The last book of the Bible, Revelation, provides sufficient identifying characteristics of the beast. It would:

Arise from the sea —"I stood upon the sand of the sea, and saw a beast rise up out of the sea." Revelation 13:1. Beasts in prophecy represent nations and kingdoms (Daniel 7:23); and the sea, or water, represents multitudes of people (Revelation 17:15). Here is pictured the papal power that emerged in densely populated, old-world Europe.

Receive its power and authority from the dragon—"The beast which I saw was like unto a leopard, and his feet were as the feet of a bear, and his mouth as the mouth of a lion: and the dragon gave him his power, and his seat, and great authority." Revelation 13:2. The dragon represents Satan working through pagan Rome. It was pagan Rome that opened the way for papal Rome to rule the world. In 330 A.D. the Roman Emperor Constantine the Great abandoned his capital, the city of Rome, and moved to Byzantium, later named Constantinople. Thus, the Bishop of Rome was free to expand his authority.

Be a world-wide religious and political power—"All that dwell upon the earth shall worship him, whose names are not written in the book of life of the Lamb slain from the foundation of the world." Revelation 13:8.

The Roman Catholic Church is a system with tremendous world-wide influence on governments and religious and secular organizations. Presently, the Vatican has 177 diplomatic ties to foreign nations. Its overt and covert efforts are aimed at regaining control of the world. At an accelerated rate, the pope is reaching out to both Protestants and non-Christians. Very soon the world will be united on the basis of commonly-held doctrines and beliefs.

Receive a deadly wound— "I saw one of his heads as it were wounded to death." Revelation 13:3. How was this fulfilled? The wound was inflicted when, in 1798, the pope was taken prisoner by Napoleon's General Berthier, and the papal influence seemed for a time to have ended. Stripped of his power, both civil and ecclesiastical, the captive pope, Pius VI, died in exile in Valence, France, on August 29, 1799. Thus, the papacy for a time lost its influence and power in world affairs.

Be healed— "His deadly wound was healed: and all the world wondered after the beast." Revelation 13:3. Prophecy also pointed to the papacy's revival and strengthening of power after its deadly wounding in 1798. In 1929 the independent Vatican reemerged. The "Supreme Pontiff" was restored to temporal power, signaling the rise of papal power—the healing of the deadly wound. On February 12, 1929, *The San Francisco Chronicle* published an article with the headline: "Mussolini and Gasparri Sign Roman Pact, ... Heal Wound of Many Years." Soon the whole world, except for a faithful remnant, will "wonder" after the beast.

Be guilty of blasphemy-- "There was given unto him a mouth speaking great things and blasphemies." Revelation 13:5. Jesus was accused by the leaders of Israel of blasphemy because He forgave people's sins. Did He have the authority to do this? Of course, because He is God. But when any other person or an organization claims the authority to forgive sins, it is blasphemous! The Roman Catholic Church admits and even boasts that it has the right to forgive sins.

Consider the following startling claim: "Seek where you will, through Heaven and earth, and you will find but one created being who can forgive the sinner.... That extraordinary being is the priest, the

Catholic priest." –*The Catholic Priest*, pp. 78, 79. Besides the counterfeit system of forgiveness by man, the Roman Catholic Church officially claims: "The Pope alone is deservedly called by the name 'Most Holy' because he is the Vicar of Christ, who is the fountain and source and fullness of all holiness." –Bill Stringfellow, *All in the Name of the Lord*, p. 115. The following blasphemy is recorded in Extracts from Lucius Ferraris, "*Papa II*" (art.), Prompta Bibliotheca, vol. 6, pp. 25–29: "The Pope is of so great dignity and so exalted that he is not a mere man, but as it were God, and the vicar of God."

Dear brothers and sisters around the world, I have some good news for you. Only God, through the blood of Jesus Christ, can—and is willing to—forgive any and all the sins we have committed. We are always welcome to go to our best and most loving friend, Jesus, today and every day in the coming New Year. He is our High Priest and Mediator. He pleads for us in the heavenly sanctuary. Let us go to Him with all our sins and in humility and contrition ask for forgiveness. His blood is all-sufficient. What a great God we serve!

Persecute God's people—"It was given unto him to make war with the saints, and to overcome them." Revelation 13:7. The war waged against the saints was terrible! At least 50 million people who believed in the Bible and did not follow church traditions perished at the hands of Rome during the Middle Ages. A faithful record is kept in heaven of the atrocities, too horrible to bear the light of day. The church has finally admitted to this persecution. "The Church has persecuted. Only a tyro [novice] in church history will deny that." –*Western Watchman*, December 23, 1908.

Reign for 1260 years—"Power was given unto him to continue forty and two months." Revelation 13:5. How do Bible students explain these forty-two months? It is a prophetic time period that can be unlocked with the key found in Ezekiel 4:6. There we find that one day in prophecy equals one literal year. It's that simple! Therefore, forty-two months equals 1260 days, or years. The Roman Catholic Church reigned supreme from 538 A.D. to 1798 A.D. Then, in 538 A.D., by the decree of Emperor Justinian, the bishop of Rome was chosen to be the head of all churches, definer of doctrines, and corrector of heretics. This papal supremacy came to an end in 1798 when the pope was dethroned and arrested.

Have the mysterious number 666— "Here is wisdom. Let him that hath understanding count the number of the beast: for it is the number of a man; and his number is Six hundred threescore and six." Revelation 13:18. How can we make sense of this number? The beast is a religio-political system that bears the number of a man—666. What man do we think of when the papacy is mentioned? Its head is the pope—right? What official title does he carry? An inscription that once appeared on the papal triple crown reads VICARIUS FILII DEI. The Catholic publication *Our Sunday Visitor*, of April 18, 1915, states: "What are the letters supposed to be in the Pope's crown, and what do they signify, if anything? 'The letters inscribed in the Pope's miter are these: Vicarius Filii Dei, which is the Latin for Vicar of the Son of God.'"

The letters in this title, when used as Roman numerals, add up to 666.

V = 5	F =0	D = 500
I = 1	I = 1	E = 0
C = 100	L =50	I = 1
A = 0	I = 1	
R = 0	I = 1	
I = 1		
U* = 5		
S = 0		

112+53+501=666

* formerly the same as V.

GOD'S MARK, OR SEAL—THE SABBATH

A seal confirms legal matters and has three elements. For instance, the President of the U.S.A. uses his presidential seal to authenticate documents. On his official seal we find his name—Barrack Obama; his title—President; and the territory over which he rules—the United States of America. Just as secular rulers have their seals of power, the God of heaven has His seal. It is found in the heart of the Decalogue. The fourth commandment contains all three elements found in a seal.

"Remember the sabbath day, to keep it holy. Six days shalt thou labour, and do all thy work: But the seventh day is the sabbath of the Lord thy God: in it thou shalt not do any work, thou, nor thy son, nor thy daughter, thy manservant, nor thy maidservant, nor thy cattle, nor thy stranger that is within thy gates: For in six days the Lord made heaven and earth, the sea, and all that in them is, and rested the seventh day: wherefore the Lord blessed the sabbath day, and hallowed it." Exodus 20: 8–11. Please note those three elements: 1. Name: the Lord; 2. His title: thy God (the Creator); 3. His territory: heaven and earth, the sea, and all that in them is.

"Moreover also I gave them my sabbaths, to be a sign between me and them, that they might know that I am the Lord that sanctify them." Ezekiel 20:12. God gave the human race the Sabbath as the sign, or mark, of His creative power and authority. He wants to place His distinctive seal upon our hearts and minds.

It is very interesting to read from a noted authority of the Roman church that Saturday is the correct day on which to worship. "If the Bible is the only guide for the Christian, then the Seventh-day Adventist is right in observing the Saturday with the Jew.... Is it not strange that those who make the Bible their only teacher should inconsistently follow in this matter the tradition of the Church?" –Conway, *Question Box*, 1903, pp. 254, 255.

The Catholic Church also has its mark of authority, a counterfeit seal, or mark, in contrast to the genuine seal of God. Let us discover this man-made mark identifying the church's authority.

THE MARK OF THE BEAST

In reply to a letter of October 28, 1895, to Cardinal Gibbons, asking if the church claimed the change of the Sabbath as her mark, C. F. Thomas, chancellor of the cardinal, wrote the following: "Of course the Catholic church claims that the change was her act.... And the act is a mark of her ecclesiastical power and authority in religious matters."

"Sunday is our mark of authority.... The church is above the Bible, and this transference of sabbath observance is proof of that fact." –*The Catholic Record*, London, Ontario, September 1, 1923.

Here is an explanation from the pen of inspiration that clearly reveals what it means to accept the mark of the beast: "But when Sunday observance shall be enforced by law, and the world shall be enlightened concerning the obligation of the true Sabbath, then whoever shall transgress the command of God, to obey a precept which has no higher authority than that of Rome, will thereby honor popery above God. He is paying homage to Rome and to the power which enforces the institution ordained by Rome. He is worshipping the beast and his image. As men then reject the institution which God has declared to be the sign of His authority, and honor in its stead that which Rome has chosen as the token of her supremacy, they will thereby accept the sign of allegiance to Rome—'the mark of the beast.' And it is not until the issue is thus plainly set before the people, and they are brought to choose between the commandments of God and the commandments of men, that those who continue in transgression will receive 'the mark of the beast.'" –*The Great Controversy*, p. 449.

"The change of the Sabbath is the sign or mark of the authority of the Romish church. Those who, understanding the claims of the fourth commandment, choose to observe the false sabbath in the place of the true, are thereby paying homage to that power by which alone it is commanded. The mark of the beast is the papal sabbath, which has been accepted by the world in the place of the day of God's appointment.

"No one has yet received the mark of the beast... But when the decree shall go forth enforcing the counterfeit sabbath, and the loud cry of the third angel shall warn men against the worship of the beast and his image, the line will be clearly drawn between the false and the true. Then those who still continue in transgression will receive the mark of the beast." –*Evangelism*, pp. 234, 235.

The great issue that will divide this world will be the commandments of God vs. the commandments of men. His people will not receive the mark of the beast, because they will be loyal to all the commandments, including true Sabbath worship. We are swiftly approaching the final contest that will decide our destiny.

IDENTIFYING THE IMAGE OF THE BEAST

We have identified the beast as the Roman Catholic system. Another animal, with two horns like a lamb, will be instrumental in forcing the whole world to pay homage to the Roman hierarchy, as presented in Revelation 13:11–14.

This second beast represents the United States of America, which will pattern itself after the papal power. In other words, America will resemble the first beast in its antagonistic activities toward conscientious dissenters. Here are two statements found in the Spirit of Prophecy that clearly describe who the image of the beast is and how it will use persecution to accomplish its ends.

"The 'image to the beast' represents that form of apostate Protestantism which will be developed when the Protestant churches shall seek the aid of the civil power for the enforcement of their dogmas." –*The Great Controversy*, p. 445.

"In order for the United States to form an image of the beast, the religious power must so control the civil government that the authority of the state will also be employed by the church to accomplish her own ends." —*Ibid.*, p. 443.

Apostate Protestants are today joining hands with the government in tearing down the fragile wall of separation between church and state. Soon the final battle will begin.

"When the leading churches of the United States, uniting upon such points of doctrine as are held by them in common, shall influence the state to enforce their decrees and to sustain their institutions, then Protestant America will have formed an image of the Roman hierarchy, and the infliction of civil penalties upon dissenters will inevitably result." —*Ibid.*, p. 445.

The two fundamental doctrines that unite mainline Protestant churches and the Catholic Church are the immortality of the soul and Sunday sacredness. Other divergent and controversial doctrines are lightly treated in ecumenical dialogues.

What current events point to the formation of a single world church body? Here is a portion of an article about the work of the World Council of Churches and its goal for the future:

"In the pews at St. John Chrysostom, usually a place of worship for Catholic parishioners, representatives of almost a dozen Christian denominations gathered to pray for unity among the Christian faiths. As part of the internationally held Week of Prayer for Christian Unity, Cardinal Sean O'Malley of the Catholic Archdiocese of Boston, [the] Metropolitan Methodios of the Greek Orthodox Metropolis of Boston and Rev. Diane Kessler of the Massachusetts Council of Churches led a diverse group of worshipers in the ecumenical prayer service on Jan. 24. Also represented were clergy from various religious organizations, including Lutheran, Episcopalian, Baptist and Armenian Orthodox.

"Organizers and participants hope events such as last week's service will remind members of all faiths of the importance of working toward Christ's will, which is to have one united Christian church. Organized by the World Council of Churches and the Vatican's Pontifical Council for Promoting Christian Unity, identical services were held throughout the week in churches around the world.

"'When you hear Protestants, Catholics saying the same words, you think if everybody's saying it, how are we so different?' said Terry Curran, a member of Sacred Heart Parish in Roslindale. 'It is very different from how we were brought up.' Ecumenical work between churches is done with the clear goal of one day uniting the diverse Christian denominations into one." –Alyce Nicolo, "*A Call for Unity*," Wednesday, January 31, 2007 (found on www.townonline.com/roslindale/homepage/8998966588161916927).

Not only is the World Council of Churches active in promoting unity among churches, but the Moral Majority and the Lord's Day Alliance in America also have strong voices in legislative councils. The desire of these groups is to bring people back to God, back to prayer, and back to church. They realize that there needs to be a spiritual awakening among Americans. A strong appeal for Sunday worship is made by these organizations.

Other significant factors that help set the stage for a national Sunday law are the intensifying threat of terrorist attacks, the escalating crime rate, and the abortion crisis, as well as political corruption and terrible calamities of nature.

Advocates of a Sunday law believe a weekly day of rest would help restore stability and order to families and society as a whole. It may sound like a good idea, but it will lead to the loss of civil and religious freedom. Are we ready to face the consequences of a Sunday law? It has been predicted by the Word of God, and it will surely come to pass.

"And he had power to give life unto the image of the beast, that the image of the beast should both speak, and cause that as many as would not worship the image of the beast should be killed. And he causeth all, both small and great, rich and poor, free and bond, to receive a mark in their right hand, or in their foreheads: And that no man might buy or sell, save he that had the mark, or the name of the beast, or the number of his name." Revelation 13:15–17.

Imagine the day when the United States will turn away from its established principles of civil and religious liberty and become a dictatorship! Force will be used to coerce people to trample on the seventh-day Sabbath and honor a counterfeit day by worshiping on it. Soon you and I will not be able to buy food and other necessities for our families. Selling a car, a bicycle, furniture will be impossible.

How will we fare when our little children say, "Daddy, Mommy, I'm hungry. I want something to eat!" Will we give up our faith so that we can continue to provide for our families? How will we react when we are forced to leave our tidy apartments or comfortable homes to seek refuge in the mountains or caves? Will we leave our home—or submit to the government's demands? The need to decide will soon become a sober reality. The issue will be, Whom will we worship—God or Satan? America will not only use economic pressure but will also ultimately pass a death decree. It will be the final test for every living person on earth.

"History will be repeated. False religion will be exalted. The first day of the week, a common working day, possessing no sanctity whatever, will be set up as was the image of Babylon. All nations and tongues and peoples will be commanded to worship this spurious sabbath.... The decree enforcing the worship of this day is to go forth to all the world." *–Last Day Events*, pp. 134, 135.

"As America, the land of religious liberty, shall unite with the papacy in forcing the conscience and compelling men to honor the false sabbath, the people of every country on the globe will be led to follow her example." *–Testimonies for the Church*, vol. 6, p. 18.

The Sunday law will be enacted first in the United States of America, then will sweep over the rest of the world, and will include all communist regimes, Islamic countries, and Buddhist, Hindu, and spiritualist communities. America will work jointly with the papacy to compel peoples' consciences. This is definitely not God's method of working. God uses LOVE, not force, to draw people to serve Him.

When the Sunday law will be enforced, what are Adventists advised to do? "The light given me by the Lord at a time when we were expecting just such a crisis as you seem to be approaching, was that when people were moved by a power from beneath to enforce Sunday observance, Seventh-day Adventists were to show their wisdom by refraining from their ordinary work on that day, devoting it to missionary effort." –*Last Day Events*, pp.139, 140.

WHAT WILL WE RECEIVE—THE SEAL OF GOD OR THE MARK OF THE BEAST?

In the very last days of earth's history, the whole world will be divided into two classes—those who receive the mark of the beast and those who receive the seal of God. Everyone who is faithful to God will be with Jesus in His wonderful kingdom. Today is the time to take our stand on the side of truth and righteousness. By faith, let us accept Jesus into our hearts. He is waiting to be the Lord of our lives and to strengthen and uphold us in the final test. Only Jesus can help us to be faithful. Let us decide to go to Him today. Let us choose to serve God, as did Joshua:

"If it seem evil unto you to serve the Lord, choose you this day whom ye will serve; whether the gods which your fathers served that were on the other side of the flood, or the gods of the Amorites, in whose land ye dwell: but as for me and my house, we will serve the Lord." Joshua 24:15.

If we remain faithful to God and receive His seal, we will receive a glorious reward. "I saw as it were a sea of glass mingled with fire: and them that had gotten the victory over the beast, and over his image, and over his mark, and over the number of his name, stand on the sea of glass, having the harps of God." Revelation 15:2.

May the Lord be gracious to us and give us strength to be faithful in the final battle!

America and the Sunday Law

Revelation 13:11, "And 1 beheld another beast coming up out of the earth, and he had two horns like a lamb, and he spoke as a dragon."

According to Bible prophecy, the greatest crisis in the history of this world is just before us. A decree will be passed by the governments threatening economic boycott and death to those who refuse to worship the image of the beast. The following prophetic words will soon become a reality: "And he had power to give life unto the image of the beast, that the image of the beast should both speak, and cause that as many as would not worship the image of the beast should be killed. And he causeth all, both small and great, rich and poor, free and bond, to receive a mark in their right hand, or in their foreheads: And that no man might buy or sell, save he that had the mark, or the name of the beast, or the number of his name." Revelation 13:15-17.

There is no getting around it: every person living during earth's last hours will be faced with the decision either to obey God or to worship another power.

Those who pay homage to the beast and his image will be condemned by God and receive the seven last plagues. In Revelation 14, verses 9 and 10, we read, "If any man worship the beast and his image, and receive his mark in his forehead, or in his hand, the same shall drink of the wine of the wrath of God, which is poured out without mixture into the cup of his indignation." This is a matter of life or death. Therefore, we must know exactly what this mark is and how we can avoid it.

The mark of the beast is opposed to the seal of God. In Revelation chapter 7, verses 2 and 3, we learn that the seal of God is placed in the forehead, just as the mark of the beast is set in the forehead. Now we ask, what is the seal? If we can define and establish this point, it will help us identify the mark.

In His Word, God tells us what His sign or seal is. "Moreover also I gave them my sabbaths, to be a sign between me and them, that they might know that I am the Lord that sanctify them." Ezekiel 20:12. Here the Sabbath is called the sign of God. Is that the same as seal? Romans 4:11 shows that 'seal' and 'sign' are the very same thing, being used interchangeably in the Scripture, "And he received the sign of circumcision, a seal of the righteousness of the faith which he had yet being uncircumcised."

God said that the Sabbath is His sign or mark of authority. What does the beast say is the mark of its authority? Let us consider these words by C. F. Thomas, Chancellor of Cardinal Gibbons, in answer to a letter regarding the change of the Sabbath. "Of course, the Catholic church claims that the change was her act. And the act is a *mark* of her ecclesiastical power and authority in religious matters."

It is almost incredible that the majority of Christendom accepts and follows the traditions of a man-made institution.

Does anyone today have the mark of the beast? The answer is, "Absolutely not." But the mark of the beast will be enforced very soon.

Therefore, in mercy, God sends out His final warning to prepare people for the coming crisis. The issue of the conflict will be whether to give God the homage or whether to obey a man-made law. In Revelation chapter 14, verses 9 through 11, we read the most solemn warning ever given to mankind. "And the third angel followed them, saying with a loud voice, If any man worship the beast and his image, and receive his mark in his forehead, or in his hand, the same shall drink of the wine of the wrath of God, which is poured out without mixture into the cup of his indignation; and he shall be tormented with fire and brimstone in the presence of the holy angels, and in the presence of the Lamb: And the smoke of their torment ascendeth up for ever and ever: and they have no rest day nor night, who worship the beast and his image, and whosoever receiveth the mark of his name."

The counterfeit mark cannot be officially received until it is enforced by the two-horned beast of Revelation 13 (America). The United States of America will become a persecuting power that will pass a national Sunday law. This act will initiate other nations to follow suit. The Bible says, "...and all the world wondered after the Beast." Revelation 13:3. The whole world, except a minority of faithful souls, will observe Sunday, the child of the Papacy. Those who refuse to obey will be accused of law- breaking and of working against the state.

In order for this situation to develop, the constitution of the United States must either be altered or completely abandoned. How is this possible in a land of freedom? One way is to call for a constitutional convention. It takes 34 states to request this. As of now, 32 states are for it. Besides this movement to bring about specific changes in our fundamental laws, there are groups such as the Moral Majority, the New Liberty Federation, and the Lord's Day Alliance who have been advocating the passage of Sunday laws. The undercurrent of these voices is moving rapidly to achieve a desired goal--to get people back to going to church on Sunday.

Before me is a copy of a letter written by a Protestant minister who clearly states the intentions of Jerry Falwell of the Moral Majority. "As many of you know, I recently had a personal talk with Jerry Falwell. I read to him the quote in the 'Catholic Twin Circle' which says that we should petition the President and Congress for a national Sunday law. I asked questions about his views on this subject and about President Reagan. He told me that he goes along with it, and indicated that he is willing to 'fight' for Sunday. He has said in the past, 'I have a divine mandate to go right into the halls of Congress and fight for laws to save America.'"

The coercive Sunday law will seem to be the solution to the awful problems facing the U.S.A. "It will be declared that men are offending God by the violation of the Sunday sabbath; that this sin has brought calamities which will not cease until Sunday observance shall be strictly enforced.

"Those who honor the Bible Sabbath will be denounced as enemies of law and order, as breaking down the moral restraints of society, causing anarchy and corruption, and calling down the judgments of God upon the earth." *The Great Controversy*, pp. 590, 592.

God's elect will soon be accused of causing the tidal waves of lawlessness, natural catastrophes, and political corruptions. Consider, for a moment, the following headline which appeared in the *Newsweek* magazine, February 9, 1987: "Urban Murders: On the Rise; The Drug Crisis." Is not this headline alarming? Isn't the public willing to try to find a remedy for these two major problems--drugs and crime?

In addition to these concerns, many people are outraged and shocked by all the scandals involving political leaders. America is experiencing one crisis after another. Where is it all leading to? What next?

For the Protestant churches, the solution will be to enact a Sunday law to counteract all these evils. According to Revelation 13:11 -16, the Protestant churches in America will be instrumental in exalting the Papal Sabbath (Sunday) and waging war against Sabbath (Saturday) keepers.

Yes, religious freedom will be taken away. Persecution will raise its ugly head again.

"Some time ago, the President of the Lord's Day Alliance was on nation-wide T.V. This sincere man said, 'We aim to put Sunday worship on the same basis exactly as the seventh-day Sabbath was in the days of the children of Israel.' Someone, obviously shocked by this statement, spoke up and said something to the effect that back in the days of Israel they were under a theocracy, and not a democracy. They reminded the speaker that under certain circumstances in the old days when a man broke the Sabbath he was put to death (as well as for breaking the other commandments, such as committing murder.) Then the person asked the guest this question: 'Do you mean that you want to go that far...if a person doesn't keep Sunday, he'll be put to death?' The religious leader said, 'That's exactly what I mean. That's what we"re asking for!'" *National Sunday Law*, by Jan Marcussen, pp. 52-53.

"The Protestants of the United States will be foremost in stretching their hands across the gulf to grasp the hand of spiritualism; they will reach over the abyss to clasp hands with the Roman power; and under the influence of this three-fold union, this country will follow in the steps of Rome in trampling ON the rights of conscience." *The Great Controversy*, p. 588.

The above quotation clearly indicates that Protestant America will trample on the rights of conscience and will unite with spiritualism and Romanism.

One instance when the hand of unity reached over the abyss was when the U. S. government established diplomatic ties with the Vatican. The bond that will eventually end in a forced Sunday law is becoming closer and stronger. Today the ecumenical movement is taking giant steps for Christendom to achieve full unity.

More than ever before, we need to draw closer in unity with Christ rather than be involved in state-church unity. With this in mind, won't we choose to obey God and keep the true Sabbath now and in the coming and final crisis?

Who Will Rule The World In The Future?

Wouldn't it be intriguing to catch a glimpse of the future--to see what the next world empire will be? Will it be Japan? Could it be the rising new giant--China? Perhaps it will be the affluent and powerful United States of America?

Let's look in the Bible at the prophetic book of Daniel, that fascinating book that deals with the past, the present, and the future. Daniel 2 tells about the kingdom that is soon to rule the world. Let's look at this chapter in more detail.

About 2,500 years ago, Nebuchadnezzar, king of Babylon, had an unusual dream. He could not remem¬ber the contents of this dream, yet it left a powerful impression on him. He, therefore, summoned the magicians, the astrologers, the sorcerers, and the Chaldeans of his realm to help him recall and interpret the forgotten dream. They were, of course, unable to relate the dream to the king, thus showing themselves to be what they really were--deceivers.

There was someone, however, who could help the king: a young Hebrew captive Daniel. God, working through Daniel, gave King Nebuchadnezzar an important message.

What was this dream that the king forgot? Let's read about it in verses 31-35. "Thou, O king, sawest, and behold a great image. This great image, whose brightness was excellent, stood before thee; and the form thereof was terrible. This image's head was of fine gold, his breast and his arms of silver, his belly and his thighs of brass, his legs of iron, his feet part of iron and part of clay. Thou sawest till that a stone was cut out without hands, which smote the image upon his feet that were of iron and clay, and brake them to pieces. Then was the iron, the clay, the brass, the silver, and the gold, broken to pieces together, and became like the chaff of the summer threshingfloors; and the wind carried them away, that no place was found for them: and the stone that smote the image became a great mountain, and filled the whole earth."

Did Daniel tell the correct dream to the king? Absolutely, in every particular! But what was the significance of this dream? Nebuchadnezzar had to know.

Daniel then interpreted the dream: "Thou art this head of gold," he said. In other words, the golden head repre¬sented the Babylonian kingdom. When he heard this, the king probably smiled with satisfaction.

Babylon was truly a golden city in a golden age. The capital city seemed impregnable to enemy attack. The Babylonians had a food supply that could feed a million people for ten to twenty years.

And yet, despite its great military might, this golden kingdom was to come to an end.

Daniel again spoke to Nebuchadnezzar. "And after thee shall arise another kingdom inferior to thee." What nation conquered the Babylonians? Historians tell us that the Medes and Persians did in the year 538 B.C. (Their Empire is represented by the image's breast and arms of silver.)

As we continue our study, we find that the Medo-Persian rule of the world would also come to an end. History shows that defeat occurred at the battle of Arbela in 331 B.C., at the hands of Alexander the Great. Incidentally, although Alexander was able to conquer the then-known world in seven years, he could not conquer his own vices. Drinking, one of his biggest prob¬lems, led to his death at the age of 32.

God said further, "After thee shall arise another kingdom inferior to thee, and another third kingdom of brass, which shall bear rule over all the earth. And the fourth king¬dom shall be strong as iron" (verses 39, 40). After the battle of

Pydna in 168 B.C., the great iron kingdom of Rome began to rule the world. However, because of severe internal problems and the invasion by barbarian tribes, Rome, too, began to crumble.

Through Daniel, God said that the Roman Empire would be divided into ten parts. The ten barbarian tribes that overran and divided Rome were the Anglo-Saxons, Franks, Alemanni, Lombards, Ostrogoths, Visigoths, Burgundians, Vandals, Suevi, and Heruli. These ten divisions became the foundation of the modern nations of Europe. Note that God did not predict that Rome would be divided into six, seven, or even nine parts, but into exactly ten. Interesting, isn't it? The prophe¬cies of the Bible are always precise and reliable.

Now, what does prophecy say concerning the relationship be¬tween these ten divisions? "And whereas thou sawest iron mixed with miry clay, they shall mingle them¬selves with the seed of men: but they shall not cleave one to an¬other, even as iron is not mixed with clay" (verse 43). God's word says that no matter how hard the individual nations of Europe try to unite themselves, they will never become one world power.

Several attempts have been made in the past to this end, but they have always failed. Man will never be able to unite the nations of Europe. It cannot be done because God said so. These declarative seven words, "They shall not cleave one to another," have stopped men such as Charlemagne, Charles V, Louis XIV, Napoleon Bonaparte, Kaiser Wilhelm, and Adolf Hitler. Some have tried desperately to unite Europe through the inter¬marriage of royal lines, but have failed. Others have attempted to achieve unity through wars and conquest, but they also failed. Just as iron and clay do not mix, so the nations of Europe will never become a world empire.

Now that we have looked at the Babylonian, Medo-Persian, Greek, and Roman empires, as well as the divided nations of Europe, we again ask the question, what will be the next world empire? The answer is found in verse 44: "And in the days of these kings shall *the God of heaven set up a kingdom*, which shall never be destroyed: and the kingdom shall not be left to other people, but it shall break in pieces and consume all these kingdoms, and it shall stand *for ever*" (emphasis supplied). God Himself will establish His kingdom on this earth, and He will rule for ever and ever.

Note also verse 45: "Forasmuch as thou sawest that the stone was cut out of the mountain without hands, and that it brake in pieces the iron, the brass, the clay, the silver, and the gold; the great God hath made known to the king what shall come to pass hereafter." The stone represents the glorious kingdom of Jesus Christ. There can be no doubt that Christ will return to this earth, accompanied by all the holy angels, to set up His government. Both the righteous and the wicked will receive their rewards— either life everlasting or eternal destruction.

The stone that strikes the image on the feet will end all existing governments. Are you ready for this stupendous event? Are you ready to enter Christ's glorious kingdom? I hope so! To be ready means to fall on the Rock Jesus Christ and be broken. He loves you and wants you to be saved. Won't you commit your life to Him today!

When will the stone strike the metallic image? This event will occur while the last part of the image is still in existence, at the time when the ten kings of Europe are still reigning. When is that? Right now!

The Bible says, "Believe on the Lord Jesus Christ, and thou shalt be saved" (Acts 16:31). Salvation begins when we surrender our sinful lives to Jesus. Accepting Him as a personal Savior assures us of a place in His eternal kingdom. Wait no longer to be on the Lord's side! When He comes in the clouds of heaven, it will be too late to make a decision for Christ. Make your decision for Him today!

Countdown to Eternity

Today more than ever, people are asking the all-important question: How will the world end? Unfortunately, there are myriad answers to this question. From every part of the globe there comes yet another speculation, another theory, another prophecy...

What are some of the predictions made by scientists, environmentalists, futurologists, politicians, and simply concerned people? Here is a list of eight ideas about how civilization may end.

1. Terrorists will use nuclear and/or biological weapons to destroy life on planet Earth.

2. The depletion of the protective ozone layer in the atmosphere will allow the sun's ultraviolet rays to cause deadly skin cancers.

3. Epidemics of fatal diseases will wipe out the earth's population.

4. Because of massive deforestation, oxygen is being depleted and this will result in the asphyxiation of the human race.

5. A massive asteroid will collide with the earth and cause the annihilation of the human race.

6. Earth's overpopulation will result in scarcity of food and mass starvation.

7. Extremists will fight religious wars to purge the earth of the infidels, thus destroying everyone.

8. Lack of pure drinking water will result in massive deaths.

But the Bible alone has the true, reliable, answer to the question, "How will the world end?" "But the day of the Lord will come as a thief in the night; in the which the heavens shall pass away with a great noise, and the elements shall melt with fervent heat, the earth also and the works that are therein shall be burned up." 2 Peter 3:10.

An "invasion from outer space" is being planned by Jesus, the King of the Universe. He will come back the second time with a host of angels to conquer evil and to literally destroy this sinful world.

PROMISE OF CHRIST'S COMING

"And if I [Jesus] go and prepare a place for you, I will come again, and receive you unto myself; that where I am, there ye may be also." John 14:3.

Jesus Himself promised to return at God's appointed time to rescue those who are faithful to Him. There are about 2,500 references in the Bible to the Second Coming of Christ. In the Old Testament, for every prophecy of His first coming, there are eight prophecies predicting His second coming. Two thousand years ago, Jesus clearly made this promise: "I will come again." He has not forgotten us, and He wants to take away all the pain, suffering, misery and death. The blueprint of heaven calls for the restoration of the New Earth, where man and God will dwell in peace and happiness forever.

How Will Christ Return?

"But the day of the Lord will come as a thief in the night." 2 Peter 3:10.

Christ will come back to this earth unexpectedly, "as a thief in the night." The wicked will be totally surprised and over-whelmed. They will not be ready for this grand event. In A.D. 79, Mount Vesuvius erupted unexpectedly. The prosperous but sinful city of Pompeii was completely destroyed by this volcanic eruption. The inhabitants of this pleasure-loving city did not expect an explosion to end their lives. But the endless party that was their lives ended rather abruptly for the Pompeiians. The sudden and unexpected return of Christ will likewise find the wicked totally unprepared. No one will escape this fiery and fearful day of judgment, except those who have made Christ their Savior. "Behold, he cometh with clouds; and every eye shall see him, and they also which pierced him: and all kindreds of the earth shall wail because of him. Even so, Amen." Revelation 1:7.

Christ will appear in the same manner as He left the earth. This visible event will be witnessed by every living person. No one will miss seeing Jesus coming in the clouds of the sky. The angels accompanying Jesus will blow their trumpets to signal the deliverance of God's people from the captivity of Satan. When this heavenly invasion by Jesus occurs, the wicked will have no place to hide. Because of guilt and fear, they would rather welcome death than life.

Today is the Time to Prepare for Eternity! How can we get ready for the second coming of Christ?

1. Accept the fact that God loves us. John 3:16.

2. Recognize that we cannot save ourselves.

3. Believe that Jesus can and will save us.

4. Confess our sins to Jesus and believe that we are forgiven.

5. Claim His gift of eternal life and decide to serve Him forever.

"He that believeth and is baptized shall be saved; but he that believeth not shall be damned." Mark 16:16.

The End of the World

Thousands upon thousands of people all over the world are convinced beyond the shadow of a doubt, that some great cataclysmic event faces the world. Many are asking, what is Bible prophecy saying about the future and the end of the world?

In Matthew chapter 24, Jesus tells us that He is coming back to this earth. Verse 3 of this chapter says, "And as he sat upon the Mount of Olives, the disciples came unto him privately, saying, tell us, when shall these things be? and what shall be the sign of thy coming, and of the end of the world?"

In John 14:1-3, it says clearly, "Let not your heart be troubled: ye believe in God, believe also in me. In my Father's house are many mansions: if it were not so, I would have told you. I go to prepare a place for you. And if I go and prepare a place for you, I will come again, and receive you unto myself; that were I am, there ye may be also."

There you have it--from Jesus Himself. Jesus will be coming to this earth again. He says emphatically, "I will come again." That is a promise to you and me.

The Bible offers hope for us in this sin-sick, troubled world. There are such enormous problems that confront mankind for which human solutions cannot be found. The cure for the ills of humanity is the second coming of Christ! This message needs to be proclaimed with still greater fervor as we near end of this earth's history.

The great American evangelist Dwight L. Moody once said, "The church has had very little to say about it [the Second Advent]. Now, I can see a reason for this; the devil does not want us to see this truth, for nothing would wake up the church so much."

The return of Jesus is mentioned more than 300 times in the New Testament. In the Scriptures, there are eight times as many references to the second coming of Jesus as to the first coming.

Great men of faith such as Martin Luther, John Calvin, John Knox, John Wesley, John Milton, and others believed in the imminent return of Jesus. They all embraced this blessed hope and I hope, dear friend, that you also believe this teaching with all your heart!

How will He come?

In Revelation 1:7 we read. "Behold, he cometh with clouds; and every eye shall see him..."

Why does it say "every eye"? This indicates that it will be a literal, **visible** event. The whole world, those who are alive, will see Jesus. Both the righteous and the unrighteous, with their physical eyes, will see the King of Kings and Lord of Lords descend from heaven.

And not only Jesus will come, but all-the angelic host will follow. In Matthew 24: 30, 31 we read: "And then shall appear the sign of the Son of man in heaven: and then shall all the tribes of the earth mourn, and they shall see the Son of man coming in the clouds of heaven with power and great glory. And he shall send his angels with a great sound of a trumpet, and they shall gather together his elect from the four winds, from one end of heaven to the other."

For a time heaven will be silent, as the angels accompany their Lord to earth to sound their mighty trumpets. What do we learn from this? The second coming of Christ will also be an **audible** event.

Nowhere in the Scriptures do we find that it will be a secret appearing. The secret rapture teaching has no Biblical foundation. There will be no secret snatching away of the saints to heaven. This teaching is one of the greatest deceptions being preached today! When Jesus comes again, everyone will know about it. That means all the living, both young and old, rich and poor, free and bond.

Years ago, an inspired author wrote about this event: "The firmament appears to open and shut. The glory from the throne of God seems flashing through. The mountains shake like a reed in the wind, and ragged rocks are scattered on every side. There is a roar as of a coming tempest. The sea is lashed into fury. There is heard the shriek of a hurricane like the voice of demons upon a mission of destruction. The whole earth heaves and swells like the waves of the sea. Its surface is breaking up. Its very foundations seem to be giving way. Mountain chains are sinking. Inhabited islands disappear." –*The Great Controversy*, pp.

Can you still believe that only a few will witness the Second Coming of Jesus?

Then there are some folks who believe that Jesus has already come.

A woman came up to a preacher and asked him, "Are you the man who talks over the radio?" "Yes," he said, "I am one such man." "Do you believe that Christ's coming is literal?" she asked. "Yes," answered the man. Said she, "I wish you would come over to my town. My minister has a private séance. I will get you in for nothing. A mighty power comes. A glorious being appears. This is Jesus Christ." "Well," said the man, "I will not be there." "Why not?" Said he, "I have an old book that explains all that." He took out his Bible and read Matthew 24:26, 27, "Wherefore, if they shall say unto you, Behold, he is in the desert; go not forth: behold, he is in the secret chambers; believe it not. For as the lightning cometh out of the east, and shineth even unto the west; so shall also the coming of the Son of man be."

If someone should appear to you and even perform a miracle saying he is Jesus Christ, don't believe it. Jesus will not come in that manner but will appear in the air and be visible to the whole world.

WHY WILL JESUS COME AGAIN?

Again, we go to the Bible and turn to 1 Thessalonians. 4:16-17: "For the Lord Himself shall descend from heaven with a shout, with the voice of the archangel, and with the trump of God: and the dead in Christ shall rise first. Then we which are alive and remain shall be caught up together with them in the clouds, to meet the Lord in the air: and so shall we ever be with the Lord." Jesus comes for the purpose of raising the dead in Christ. All those who were faithful and have died since the time of Adam and Eve will be resurrected.

A miracle takes place. Millions and millions of people come out of their dusty graves. What will they look like? All come forth from their graves the same in stature as when they entered the tomb. Each saint is given a perfect body free from any taint of sin or disease. They arise with the freshness and vigor of eternal youth.

No longer will the blind man say, "I cannot see."

No longer will the deaf say, "I cannot hear."

No longer will the cripple say, "I cannot walk."

Jesus is coming to close all hospitals and to put all doctors out of business. He is coming to close the doors of all funeral parlors. What a wonderful hope, dear friend!

I don't know what ailments or sicknesses you are suffering from, but be assured that Jesus will soon give you a new body--DISEASE FREE! This is thrilling news!

Words cannot describe the joy of the redeemed on that day when Jesus returns. There will also be the joy of seeing again faithful loved ones who died years ago, for the coming of Jesus will reunite loved ones who have been separated by death. Little babies will be restored to their mothers' arms.

The glorious resurrection is just before us. Christ is the Resurrection and the Life.

Those who have never died and have been faithful will be translated and meet the Lord in the AIR. They will all travel to God's kingdom-- a space journey, traveling past the moon, the sun, and the stars without the need and restrictions of spaceships, spacesuits, and rocket power.

These words of promise are no idle tales or fantasy but words of truth from God Himself.

Sadly, the wicked will not take this space journey for they will be destroyed at the coming of Jesus. "And to you who are troubled rest with us, when the Lord

Jesus shall be revealed from heaven with his mighty angels, in flaming fire taking vengeance on them that know not God, and that obey not the gospel of our Lord Jesus Christ: Who shall be punished with everlasting destruction from the presence of the Lord, and from the glory of his power." 2 Thessalonians 1:7-9. Those who do not obey God's will, will not have part in God's eternal kingdom.

There are only two classes of people—the righteous and the unrighteous. To which class will you belong at the end of the world?

One of the most important questions that needs to be answered is this: Are you, dear friend, ready for Jesus to come?

How can you be prepared for the second coming of Jesus? It's really quite simple.

John writes in the Gospel of John, chapter 6:37, "All that the Father giveth me shall come to me; and him that cometh to me I will in no wise cast out."

I appeal to you to come to Jesus today. He understands you; He is your friend, big brother and most of all, your Savior who died for you. He loves you immeasurably. He will not reject you, if you only make that first step. Come as you are, filthy, unrighteous—a sinner in need of grace. Ask Jesus to come into your heart today. You will not regret it. It is a blessed experience to know that Jesus forgives and saves the sinner.

The time in which we are living is serious and solemn. The world cannot continue as it is much longer. It is on the verge of a stupendous crisis and the second coming of Christ.

I wish to conclude with this verse: "Christ was once offered to bear the sins of many; and unto them that look for him shall he appear the second time without sin unto salvation." Hebrews 9:28.

Let us with hope and faith and love in our hearts prepare for the greatest event in all of earth's history—the second coming of Christ.

www.ingramcontent.com/pod-product-compliance
Lightning Source LLC
Chambersburg PA
CBHW071519150726
48000CB00002B/604

9798640932355